Enthusiastic reviews for Lior Samson's novels –

### *Distant Sons*

"[A] book that will stay with me, probably for the rest of my life, and that I know I'll read again. ... It enlarged my experience of being human." *–M. Thornberg, author*

### *The Rosen Singularity*

"The plotting is ingenious and the characters come through strongly." *–Rebecca Goldstein, MacArthur Fellow, author*

### *The Millicent Factor*

"A solid page turner. The author keeps the pace just right with action and chases ... and backroom dealings." *–RJ Beam, author*

### *The Intaglio Imprint*

"Super-realism and compelling rationale, ... an intricate and incisive creation." *–George Church, geneticist*

### *The Drucker Proxy*

"An edge-of-the-seat, emotionally gripping, intimate, arousing, techno-legal tour-de-force." *–Phillip M. Samson, attorney*

### *Bashert (The Homeland Connection)*

"Samson writes with a crisp elegance, like John Le Carré, and weaves his plot magically." *–James A. Anderson, author*

### *The Dome (The Homeland Connection)*

"An excellent read, and very highly recommended." *–Midwest Book Review*

### *Web Games (The Homeland Connection)*

"This extraordinary author has the ability to anticipate events. ... You will not put it down." *–Alan Caruba, critic, BookViews*

### *Chipset (The Homeland Connection)*

"[A] multi-dimensional thriller ... populated by flesh-and-blood characters." *-Avraham Azrieli, author*

### *Gasline (The Homeland Connection)*

"[A] great novel . . . high concept, flesh-and-blood protagonist, and realistic action. ... [It] will raise your blood pressure and make you think." *–Columbia Review of Books and Film*

### *Flight Track (The Homeland Connection)*

"Stunning, compelling, thought-provoking. To the book's broad scope and expert pacing, add three-dimensional, engaging characters." *–M. Thornburg, author*

### *Exit Plans (The Homeland Connection)*

"Page-turner, nail-biter, thought-provoker [by] one of the two great American writers of near-future-maybe-as-soon-as-tomorrow fiction most worth reading ." *–M. Thornburg, author*

### *The Four-Color Puzzle*

"[A]n authentic thinking person's ideal mystery; an eloquent feast of words and an excellent story." *–Jeanie B. Clemmons, author*

### *Always Me*

"[A] captivating puzzle. I didn't dare put it down!"

*–M. Thornburg, author*

# IMAGINED POETS SILENT SONGS

Also by Lior Samson, from Gesher Press

***Distant Sons***

The Homeland Connection:
***Bashert***
***The Dome***
***Web Games***
***Chipset***
***Gasline***
***Flight Track***
***Exit Plans***

The Immortality Quartet:
***The Rosen Singularity***
***The Millicent Factor***
***The Intaglio Imprint***
***The Drucker Proxy***

***Always Me***
***Always Beginning***

***The Four-Color Puzzle***

***Requisite Variety: Collected Short Fiction***
***Death Rehearsals: Stories of Endings Dark and Bright***

Available from Amazon and other booksellers

# IMAGINED POETS SILENT SONGS

Collected Poems and Lyrics

by Lior Samson

GESHER PRESS

**Gesher Press**
Rowley, Massachusetts



5 4 3 2

ISBN 978-1-7326091-5-0

Cover and book design: Larry Constantine
Set in Aila

For Joy, my firstborn, and Tovah, my youngest —
the true poets in my life.

*Writing our story in rhyme, from here to the edges of time.*

– Larry Constantine

# Table of Contents

# Preface

I am a journalist and a novelist. In the former role, my job is to get at the facts and report on reality; in the latter, my function is to make it all up. This collection of poetry and lyrics by sundry poets and songwriters is a product of the latter process, a work of fiction based in fiction. The poems and songs by fictive characters are all reprinted from works of fiction, including in some cases from the putative authors' imaginary unpublished manuscripts. This book, then, is a layered confection of fiction, topped with a house-made frosting of still more invention.

Poems are generally expected to stand on their own, yet each entry in this volume was originally embedded in a story and has been extracted from that context. To allow the reader to experience each work independent of its backstory but also to understand something of the storyline with which it was originally entwined, notes about the fictive poets and songwriters and the context in which their work was originally quoted can be found after the selections. These, too, are fiction, purely a product of my imagination, which makes them no less real.

In the interest of full disclosure, I am also a fiction. In reality, I am actually someone else. In reality, I am deeply indebted to my wife, Lucy, who first encouraged my quixotic impulses to embed poetry in prose and then supported me in this equally quixotic project. And I am also grateful to my daughter Tovah, for teaching me to rap—or at least do an over-the-hill approximation—and to understand some of the subtler elements of spoken-word poetry.

# IMAGINED POETS SILENT SONGS

# Part 1 - Poetry in Prose

Yes, this is a book of poetry, and yes, what you are reading is not a poem. Behind the poems here collected is a story—many stories, in truth—and the connections between the poetry and the prose are important, beginning with the question of why. Why would poetry be written into works of contemporary narrative fiction?

I am a storyteller. I write popular and genre fiction, writing with intention, striving for authenticity, and seeking to engage readers in an experience that both entertains and provokes. I want to leave readers with a lingering aftertaste, like the long satisfying finish that follows a swallow of a fine wine. I want to leave them thinking about what they have read. As of this writing, I have fifteen novels and two collections of short fiction in print. Like the flourish of the artist's initials nestled in the lower corner of an oil painting, a subtle signature of my fiction has been the inclusion of poetry embedded in the narrative.

Before there was the written word, storytellers of old committed to memory lengthy legends and extended storylines, passing on their cultural and literary heritage aided by rhyme and rhythm, alliteration and allegory. If there were distinctions drawn between poetry and prose, the boundaries were likely to have been blurry at best.

In the minds of most modern readers, poetry, whether spoken or sung, and narrative fiction, from short stories to novels, are rather distinct and separate forms, yet there have always been the means to mix them. Both are rooted in that same ancient, preliterate soil, when stories were rhymed and chanted as mnemonic mechanisms that made it easier to stay true to tradition—or to interpolate invention.

Poets may try their hand at prose, and novelists may dabble in poetry, and some writers remain never quite sure who they are or what they want to do when they grow up. I am an honorary member of this last tribe. Like so many of us with creative leanings, a young me filled yellow foolscap pads and three-ring notepaper with impassioned and imaginative poems whelmed with angst and profundity, overloaded with showy vocabulary, and layered with obscure imagery. Fortunately, almost none of that juvenilia survives extant.

What did survive is an impulse, an impulse that morphed and matured as I built my craft as a writer. As I learned to write—first through articles, then columns, and on to book-length treatises, and finally from short stories to full-length fiction—that love of the poetic continued to burn beneath the surface.

Of course, a writer does not have to choose between poetry and prose. There are many means to mix the literary streams, and some of the best writers draw on both branches or continue to find inventive ways to comingle the two. Vladimir Nabokov's brilliant and eccentric *Pale Fire* springs to mind. But experimental literary forms and radical techniques that defy categorization in their melding of the poetic and the narrative are not my thing as a novelist, nor have I taken up such well-worn synthetic techniques as the prose poem or prosimetrium. My signature flourish is a far simpler and less daring one, embedding the occasional poem as an integral element of the narrative storyline.

Why? Because poems and poetry—whether spoken, written, or sung—are part of ordinary, everyday life for most people. We send greeting cards to each other with doggerel rhymes; on holidays and special occasions, we sing traditional words to established melodies; we sing along to the lyrics of our favorite popular songs; we quote clichéd lines of famous poetry in casual conversation; or we read aloud a compelling couplet to our partners. Poetry and song are simply part of life, and honest fiction recognizes this quotidian reality.

❧ ❧

The conscious decision to make this use of poetry a signature element of my narrative fiction came with my first novel, *Bashert.* My wife, Lucy, an award-winning writer herself, tends to be brutally (and usefully) critical of my early drafts, but in this case she singled out for rare praise a poem, "This Uncertain Road," quoted by one of my central characters. She asked me where it came from, who wrote it, and I told her that it was by Barry Markham, another character in the book, an imagined poet.

The poets and lyricists, singers and songwriters who are the authors of the works reprinted here are, like the other denizens of my novels, fully-imagined characters, and once I come to know them, I leave them free to write in their chosen idioms and personal styles, just as I let them speak their lines with their own voices. Classicist Clarkson Hargrove, writer of young-adult epic fantasy, does not write poetry in the style of free-spirit singer-songwriter Denton Reynolds nor in the energetic rhythms of rap-metal fusion artists Chaim Hassan and Abdullah Sirhan. Just because I make them up does not mean these poets and lyricists are not real. Even when their performances are off-stage, they have been key to the storylines I have imagined and shared with readers.

In this first section are assembled the poetry from my prose in its purest form, poems written by diverse poets, all of them inextricably linked with me. In the second section, with its own introduction, are original song lyrics from that same well-spring. I hope that at least some of these speak to you, and that they leave on the palate an "aftertaste, robust and clear," that they prod your mind to ponder or wonder. And, if the impulse strikes, share them again. That is what poetry and stories are about.

## *This Uncertain Road*

Barry Markham

This road ahead I do not know.
I know not into what valleys
Or past what shadows it may
lead,
But I will walk with you,
Beloved,
Along its wide turns and
through its straits.
Whatever course,
Through storms and lulls,
I will go.
Even to the ends of the Earth,
Even to the end of life,
I will go.

And I will keep watch, my Fated
One.
I will straighten the road or
change the course
of rivers.
For you, I will rewrite the words
of Fate.

## About the Poet

**Barry Markham**, is a British-American shoe designer and frequent contributor to South Florida Rainbow Reflections, a quarterly chapbook compilation of LGBTQ+ poetry and short fiction. The poem, "This Uncertain Road," was written for the wedding of his sister, sculptor and jewelry designer Shira Markham, to Migdal Rozeyn (born Mitchell Rossing), an American immigrant to Israel having a history of unsanctioned operations with international repercussions.

From *Bashert* (Gesher Press, 2010), reprinted with permission.

## *At the Battle of Harjhan*

Clarkson Hargrove

And the poet chanted the words
spoken by the king to the dying
prince:

In your arm, carried you my
sleeping tomorrows,
a sword of my destiny and yours,
a gleaming edge of hope against
the sweeping sorrows of ugly
dreams
and fantasies of other planes that
neither here nor elsewhere lie.
Resolute, you raised your blade,
and into battle rode.

And fought you well, my first-
born son,
but on the Plain of Harjhan, on
this plane,
the only one we know or ever
shall,
bought you well that bitter bolt,
flung from an evil cross,
a bow of false beliefs in other
gods than we, imagined higher
beings.
And now 'tis I who is seeing, as
one such creature comes, the
specter of my very certainty
that this and all is all and for
eternity.
The specter speaks,
With my own voice declares:

I am the night, approaching
from the east.
I am the dark truth,
unchallenged, unappeased.
I am the cold cloak, the timeless
shroud, the dry wind that
steals the breath.
I am reality, I am finality. I am
death.

## About the Poet

**Clarkson Hargrove**, a British professor of Medieval Literature and Philosophy of Science and a Life Member of the Radical Association for Atheist and Agnostic Action, is the author of the best-selling ten-volume young-adult epic fantasy, *The Princes of Pelucida.* He recited an excerpt from this poem as he himself lay dying.

From *The Dome* (Gesher Press, 2010), reprinted with permission.

## *If But There Were More Time*

Karl Lustig

If but there were more time
And lives to lead
  And lines to follow leading up,
Then I could love you, too.
But here we stand,
  Our footprints traced across
  the wetted sand
  Already fading in a rising tide.
And life afar, and with another,
  so deeply etched inside,
  Reaches out across the gulf
  within.
The shore's chaotic and unsteady
  wind

Now lifts unspoken whispers
And sweeps them from the
scene,
Leaving only sand and silence
In the salt-strewn space that
lies between.
If but for this—
and all the world—
Then I could love you, too.

## About the Poet

**Karl Lustig**, a Michigan-born immigrant to Israel, is a technology writer and consultant with a penchant for intrigue. He quotes the poem, "If But There Were More Time," to a Destiny Allen, a woman he has become friends with. Too embarrassed to admit he wrote it himself while still a student in college, he claims to have forgotten the author of the poem.

From *Web Games* (Gesher Press, 2010), reprinted with permission.

## *Saudade: The Homeland Connection*

Julianna Nowack Ryesdale Lustig

Like spider silk that spans the
path
From one unnoted branch to
another—
or to nowhere—
Gossamer steel adrift,
Seen only when obliquely lit
by chance illumination.
Yet, it remains to snare the
unaware,
Clinging: *saudade*,
the homeland connection.

In the lonely sighs of winds on
distant sails,
In remembered poems, repainted
scenes,
The retelling of time-distorted
tales: *saudade*.
A homesick ache that links us to
impersonal pasts,
The hope to be at home at last,
Whether we are here or
elsewhere still unreached:
the homeland connection.
We travel in the faith that we are
free,
Yet it trails behind us, to teach
us of
Its sticky trace as strong as love.

## About the Poet

**Julianna Nowack Ryesdale Lustig**, mother of Karl Lustig, was born in Poland and escaped to England as a teenager during the Nazi occupation. Having spent time in neutral Portugal on her circuitous route to England, she riffs in this poem, handwritten on the back of a letter, on the Portuguese word *saudade*, meaning "an acute and melancholic longing for a lost homeland."

From *Chipset* (Gesher Press, 2012), reprinted with permission.

## *61398: Natural Gas*

J. Smithers "Smitty" Jackson

Whirlwind under earth,
Foul breath of long-dead
  swamps;
Above: dragon wind.

## *Gospel Choir*

J. Smithers "Smitty" Jackson

Girls in lavender
Rapping songs of salvation:
Early-onset dementia.

## *Clandestine Halftone*

J. Smithers "Smitty" Jackson

It is a mystery written in India
ink on black velvet;
A story whispered amidst a
windstorm;
A play enacted by imposters with
masks over their disguises.
It is blinding high-beam
headlights
approaching over the hill out of
the setting sun,
Elongating dark lines on the road
behind:

Within each beam, a searchlight,
Within each umbra, a shadow.
Beside the roadway, rows of
  windows close,
the curtains are drawn:
Behind each curtain a shade,
Behind each shade a blind.
Now blinded, we see nothing.
We watch in darkness and listen
  in silent assent,
Reading meaning into
  nothingness
And taking nothing away.
But we leave.
We feel our way through gray
  fog spreading
over what road remains,
Walking in half-light that is
  neither bright nor night

And within which the rich
gradations of living are
illumined.
We abandon the alabaster
and leave the blackness behind.
We are left observing a halftone
image:
An illusion in ink, dots and
blobs,
out-of-focus grays,
But strangely beautiful,
comforting.

## About the Poet

**J. Smythers "Smitty" Jackson** is an African-American industrial automation engineer. With a love of oriental languages and fluent in both Japanese and Mandarin, his preferred form is haiku. The poem "61398: Natural Gas" is an obscure insider reference to a unit of the Chinese army. His longer poem, "Clandestine Halftone," a house gift to friends in Canada, was written in reaction to his immersion in the hall-of-mirrors worlds of espionage and the clandestine services.

From *Gasline* (Gesher Press, 2012), reprinted with permission.

## *Footprints*

Eliyahu Hanavi

I will not retreat in silence.
Let the shofar sound at last
its plangent call, both sweet and
  shrill,
one long and final blast, *tekkiah
  gadolah.*
Remind the echoing hills
that we were here and passed
  before,
And left our footprints in the
  winding streets and dusty
  stalls,

and scratched our marks, still
incomplete,
Upon the city's sun-hued walls.

## About the Poet

**Eliyahu Hanavi** is the pseudonym of a transgender schoolteacher and poet living in Tel Aviv. His songs and poetry echo the theme that "we are here, and we always have been." He is quoted by mathematical biologist Rosen David at a turning point in his own life.

From *The Rosen Singularity* (Gesher Press, 2011), reprinted with permission.

## *Dark Forest*

Hidalgo Spinoza e Laredo

Dark forest, bright tutor, show
me a path,
the secret math
of counting stones and steps
unknown
until the turning point is reached.
With leafy fingers point me
down the road,
the rock-hard trail
where once I failed to learn what
others failed to teach.
Teach me to listen with
uncovered heart

to the silenced part within the
noise:
the whisper of the rising sun,
the soundless ticking of
impending death,
the echoes unending of my own
doubt.
Let me learn to see by darkened
beams
to find hidden routes out,
the unspoken dreams in
shadowed uncertainty.
Spread above me your canopy of
indifferent caring,
that I may be sheltered
as I stand staring into emptiness,
from darkness still learning,
always learning,
still.

## *Internet Pause*

Hidalgo Spinoza e Laredo

Bound by skeins of gossamer
  glass,
Digital veins of captive
  sunbeams cast
across the seas,
Bright bit-streams passed
between the rejoined absent:
Alone, together,
in the silent finite present.

## About the Poet

**Hidalgo Spinoza e Laredo** is a bilingual journalist writing for the English-language Valley Free Press newspaper in Mbutsu City in the West African nation of Busanyu. In “Dark Forest,” he writes of the lessons learned from the surrounding rain-forest as a metaphor for the demands of the city-world around him. His poem “Internet Pause” reflects on a moment of electronically connected disconnection over great distance.

From *The Millicent Factor* (Gesher Press, 2016), reprinted with permission.

## *I Imagine You, and Often*

Jakob Oster

I imagine you, and often.
Memories fade. Images of such
  clarity can only be of my own
  invention, yet they return,
  always unchanged.
You are coming up the back
  stairs wearing that silly cap
  that my mother insisted upon.
You look up to see me above, and
  your expression changes, your
  eyebrows form gentle slopes
  with the faintest crease
  between — a question,
  wondering.

What did I want?
Yes, what indeed did I want. As
if you didn't already know.
Or you are walking on the path
by Lake Como, your auburn
braids coiled at the back.
A late June breeze that is at once
both cool and warm plays with
stray wisps of hair around your
face.
You catch me studying your
profile against the bright gray
of a morning fog that has not
yet burned off, and you turn,
flashing me a smile, enigmatic,
as if you withheld a secret
from me but already burned to
share it.

And, of course, there was that
first time, and then, too, it was
your hair,
...
haloed by the sunlight, that I first
noticed: thick, like the fur of
some arctic animal, defiantly
wavy, strands of it escaping all
attempts at containment.
You stood in the vestibule, your
gaze lowered just enough to be
respectful, your hair pulled
back, emblematic of your
readiness to work with
deference and efficiency.
These traits, I would learn, would
abide through all your days.

## About the Poet

**Jakob Oster**, an American newspaper man living in the first half of the twentieth century, kept journals filled with love and longing, with stories of his personal and professional struggles and his long road home to the woman to whom he had pledged himself. He did not write poetry as such, but his style was often poetic, and the eccentric format in which he penned his entries, as in the passage quoted here, suggest that he was not unaware of the short distance between his prose and the poems they approached.

From *Distant Sons* (Gesher Press, 2019), reprinted with permission.

## *I Will With Bittersweet*

Lior Samson

Even over the hill, the birds will
  cry their joy
and fill the wind and breezes
  toying with the trees.
What greens this planet has to
  please,
grass and trees that pummel the
  eye with verdant luxury.
And fall, when Nature dies,
But death does not come quietly.
In one last joyful surge
She sets the sky ablaze,
As if to say:

I live, I die,
But, happy to have lived, I fly
Once more through windswept
 seas of airy rapture.
Yet, I will with bittersweet
 depart this world I loved so
 much—
And God, oh God, how deep I
 loved—
long embracing hours and years,
the burning color of fresh air,
the aftertaste robust and clear.
Yes, I will with bittersweet:
the sweet for all the sweet before
and not-sweet for the sweet no
 more.

## About the Poet

**Lior Samson** is an American novelist best known for his geopolitical techno thrillers, particularly the seven novels collectively known as The Homeland Connection. This poem, from one of his two collections of short fiction, is quoted by Eduardo Ribiera, an American engineer of Portuguese descent, who rediscovers reasons to live after suffering a devastating series of losses.

From "Keeping the Faith" in *Death Rehearsals* (Gesher Press, 2019), reprinted with permission.

## *Double Sunset on Melem*

Delaware E. Jackson

The wearied arid Twins descend.
As one, Melduu and Meltaa bend
To take
Small sips, a day-long thirst to
slake.
Then deeper from the placid lake
Of sand,
Of crimson runnels fanned
In waves that flood and flare and
break
Upon the drinkers. Drenched
In orange fluorescent spray,
And still unquenched,
They find too late,

The measure of their thirst too
great,
And drown to end
The day.

## *Dance with a Sun-Child*

Delaware E. Jackson

We danced around
A tracery of feathered lines,
A sketch unrolled
In twilight's cold.
Young friend of doubled golden
light,
What meaning has the gulf of
years between us
Beside the awesome, star-draped
night
I crossed,
Only then to wander, lost
With you in forenoon's heat,
And found in you as night designed?

You've yet to meet
What lies betrayed
Within my aging mind;
Still, teaching me of laughter
   played
Like dancing games,
With eyes of golden flames,
You see the dance unwind.

## About the Poet

**Delaware E. Jackson** is an Earth-trained African-American on an extended mission to the double-star planet Melem, selected in part because of his resemblance in height and skin color to the i-Mel, natives of that world. "Double Sunset on Melem" was written in the early weeks after his arrival on the desert planet. "Dance with a Sun-Child" is a much later reflection on his friendship with a young i-Mel.

From "Deaths Children" in *Death Rehearsals* (Gesher Press, 2019), reprinted with permission.

## *Kids at School*

Jamal Shirley, age 7

Ugly, cute.
Pretty, plain.
Faces, stories.
Different, same.

## *Chalk Lines*

Jamal Shirley, age 9

I think lots.
I think in squares.
Sidewalk chalk lines hold my
  thoughts.
Hopscotch in the air.
Can I cross those lines I draw?

## About the Poet

**Jamal Shirley**, the mixed-race son of restaurateur Darlene Shirley and police detective Randall McMurphy, showed a poetic and philosophical bent from a very young age. Raised by his mother in Jamaica Plain, Massachusetts, he was shot and killed at the age of nine, the accidental victim of a youth gang drive-by shooting. His poems, "Kids at School" and "Chalk Lines" were supplied from memory by his father.

From *Always Me* (Gesher Press, 2020), reprinted with permission.

## *Birdstrike*

Abigail van der Houten

A nameless bird flies
into a clouded sky
painted by reflected lies
in glass, a crystal void already
filled.
Stunned, she falls, is stilled,
then rises, shaken,
to chase a different light.

I wander an unfenced landscape,
prison grounds without escape,
and walk toward a wood that
promises a path,
but deadfalls block the way.

I turn, mistaken,
to chase a different dark.

## About the Poet

**Abigail van der Houten**, the young wife of Professor Gareth Belknap of Holcomb University, kept a diary in which she recorded, sometimes in poetry, the depths of her joys and miseries. Her poem "Birdstrike" speaks of her sense of privileged imprisonment. She disappeared from the university campus under mysterious circumstances, an apparent victim of abduction and murder.

From *Always Me* (Gesher Press, 2020), reprinted with permission.

## *Always Beginning:*

### *Reflections on Life After a New Year*

Martine Rossum
Rosh Hashanah, 5767

Life after, awaking from a dream into
  the dream, the drama of You,
  calling out to You
  after falling out with You.
Are You still there? Or are You here?
Are things as they seem to You?
Or are You as things seem to me?

I know this place, this loom of woven
  thought,
  cobweb draped, the room You once
  escaped

before I even noted You were sought.
A store for tomes unbought, an
antiquarian preserve of memoirs and
vignettes,
triumphs and regrets,
arcana of the self
successively arrayed but unarranged.
On one low shelf, there rests the book I
penned,
the paper, parchment-like with age,
yet half each page remains unprinted
yet.
I know too well how it begins but
nothing of the end.

On its half-title page, I strain to read a
two-line title halved:
on one line, Life;
on one line, After.

After what, I ask myself. After that, I
answer.

The book is signed, a dedicated brief:
To Me,
I hope you find anticipated peace.
From Me, forever yours.
This slim collection, a juried selection,
the only extant copy of a first
edition—
What is its worth, this soul-bearing
history?
What would it bring if sold, what if
abandoned to the earth?
A mystery.

Already text is blurred and ink is
smudged
from readings yet unheard,

unviewed but not unjudged,
marked up by marginalia and riddled with redaction,
as if the reader—or the writer—
still struggled to sort out the story's action.
True.

But truth evolves.
Some beginnings are lost, others revised at some cost until unrecognized,
forgotten but memorized as told and retold to the end.
Then.

Do we rise awake or fall for Time asleep?
Are we tossed like refuse bulldozed

into stinking heaps,
transfer-station limbos,
before becoming landfills
piled to the sky?
Are we more? Is there more?
And why?

From the first place I read first words:
In the beginning, it states.
The folio is numbered third, but here
bound first, a quirk,
as is a custom of the trade, even in
self-published work.

Who remembers their beginning stage,
earliest years:
the screams, the scramble,
laughing terror, sudden tears,
discovery, recovery,

the climb to be at cause,
to rise and walk without a tumble?
Up the stairs?
To where?

Recalled or not, beginnings still
survive, arrive,
starting over and again:
reiteration, reprise without repeat,
always beginning, another beginning
for as long as we feel
we reach to be real, to be alive.

Beginnings. Plural.
But in the end. Singular.

The end: a singularity.
Along the spiral path we lead, we plead
for clarity:

renewal, a seed, the offer of
redemption that heeds the Head
of each new year—
if only we can summon true
intention, resuming self-invention
that we be rewritten here
once more into The Book.

Another turn, another day, we look into
another chance,
another rightful choosing,
until that one and single end.
Until that then, until that loosing,
we advance:
Always beginning.

## *Rock Rolling Downhill*

Martine Rossum

Dislodged in mischief and out of
 boredom,
a once-settled stone, a small boulder,
begins its downhill roll, plunging into
its unseen fate already marked,
from the starting gate
a race toward a future dark
but known,
its trajectory predictable.
The witnesses, like us, believe they can
 project its story,
 but this conclusion
 is arrogant illusion.
The unplanned path has no solution.

The math's abstract and incomplete,
 the stone, concrete.
No perfect sphere,
 this mineral aggregate,
 misshapen, oblate, hollowed and
 hilled.
It reaches a gully unwilled and bobs
 and careers,
 bounces and veers,
 kissing other rocks along the way.
Stone chips fly.
Striker and struck are both reshaped
 with each
 collision:
 deflected, diverted,
 detoured without decision,
launching other pebbles becoming
 tumbling rebels
unled along unfollowed histories;

each final resting space, location and
circumstance
determined only by chance, mysteries
until that moment of stasis restored.
Above, the watchers stand, no longer
bored.

## About the Poet

**Martine Rossum** was an art historian whose love of art and its origins ultimately led her into the slow and sometimes painful discovery of the perplexing past of her father, celebrated robotics pioneer Abel Rossum. A prolific but unpublished poet, her poem "Always Beginning," appeared for the first time in print in a tribute book produced for the Jewish High Holy Days. "Rock Rolling Downhill" was an early work inspired by a challenge from a creative writing instructor about how not to plot a story.

From *Always Beginning* (Gesher Press, 2021), reprinted with permission.

# Part 2 - Lyrics in Literature

Nearly everyone sings. Song is a pervasive part of the ordinary life of people around the globe. In modern Western cultures, we are surrounded by popular music and immersed in lyrics streaming from our smartphones and blasting from satellite radio in our cars. Contemporary cinema certainly reflects this playlist culture, but written fiction does not always. There is a reason for that.

Song lyrics and poetry pose a problem for writers of fiction. Under current copyright laws and conventions, even the quotation of a single line can constitutes a violation of copyright. Technically, the author must obtain written permission from the copyright holder or risk facing a cease-and-desist order or lawsuit.

In practice, obtaining formal permission may be all but impossible, especially for indie authors or small-press publishers. If it is even possible to track down and contact the copyright holder or its agent, permission may often be denied or offered only at a prohibitive fee. One author in a chat group lamented that to quote a single line from a popular song he would have had to pay £1200, a sum that probably exceeded what he would ever earn from royalties on his small-press novel.

❧ ❧

*The Four-Color Puzzle* was my first foray into the mystery genre, but like so much of my writing, it plays loose with conventions and blurs boundaries, with a double love story and elements of techno thriller thrown into the mix. The edgy storyline explores the special and often fraught relationship between teacher and student, raising questions about boundaries and interdependence, ethics and responsibilities. I originally had thought about quoting some lines from the Phil Collins song in the Disney animated feature, "Tarzan"—you know the ones—but obtaining actual permission proved to be practically impossible and financially out of the question.

Then I reminded myself that I'm a novelist. What I do is make things up. So, as a piece of the backstory, I invented singer-songwriter Denton Reynolds, a New England folk-rock artist and one-hit wonder with a song called "Teachable Moments" whose lyrics are quoted by characters in the novel. I actually wrote the song, not just a couple of lines of lyrics, and decided to include the backstory and the complete lyrics in an appendix. I had intended to include a lead sheet with the actual music, but that proved too difficult to do within publishing constraints. Someday.

Readers liked the cultural footnote to the story that the appended song provided, so I used the technique again in four other novels.

❧ ☙

My connections with music run, if possible, even deeper than with poetry. In my youth, I studied violin, saxophone, and piano, although I never developed much in the way of performance skills, I learned to read music and to appreciate how it was constructed. Music, especially singing, was just there, part of the ambience of my growing up.

As a young adult, I indulged in penning the occasional folksong, and, when my first children were born, wrote original lullabies for each of them. None of this music was ever published or performed outside the home, but the songs became part of family folklore and tradition.

In midlife, encouraged by a friend who was also a singer and songwriter, I started studying theory and composition at the New England Conservatory. This was a life-changing experience, not alone for what I was learning. At a piano recital by one of my professors, I met his father, an orchestra and choir conductor. By the end of the evening, I had secured a commission for my first orchestral work. That work I parlayed into a second commission for an original choral work, followed over the years by other works for chorus and instrumental ensemble.

For music to make its way into my narrative fiction should surprise no one.

## *Teachable Moments*

Denton Reynolds

When the teacher becomes the student
And the classroom is the hall,
Then the teachings of philosophy
Must be rewritten on the wall.

So the scholars must relearn the primer,
As the lessons of their youth grow dimmer.
Still the pupils spy a hopeful glimmer
Down dark corridors of insight.
(Down dark corridors of insight.)

(chorus)
Teach, that you may learn again,
And learn that you might teach me.
In the answers of your questioning,
May your someday wisdom reach me.
(repeat)

Once I knew my own direction,
And for fortune I was bound.
Then there was no place for divinity
Or distractions to be found.

But you taught me I was just a
  beginner
On a journey where no one is the
  winner,
And the lines to follow keep getting
  thinner
On the fading map of insight.

(On the fading map of insight.)

(chorus)
Teach, that you may learn again,
And learn that you might teach me.
In the answers of your questioning,
May your someday wisdom reach me.
(repeat)

The teachable moments hide
unheeded
In the twisted turns of time.
And the stanzas spin to infinity
In rewoven words of rhyme.

So we read our bibles cover-to-
cover
For the timeless truth we hope to
recover

And quotations we recite to each
  other
In elusive lines of insight.
(In elusive lines of insight.)

(chorus)
Teach, that you may learn again,
And learn that you might teach me.
In the answers of your questioning,
May your someday wisdom reach me.
(repeat)

Out of echoes of our epiphanies,
From the narratives never taught,
We draft our discordant destinies,
And we forge a future fraught.

We feign indifference to resistance

As we signal strangers over the
distance,
Marking out a mutual path of
persistence
In synthetic signs of insight.
(In synthetic signs of insight.)

(chorus)
Teach, that you may learn again,
And learn that you might teach me.
In the answers of your questioning,
May your someday wisdom reach me.
(repeat)

## *Always Me*

Denton Reynolds

A shade from the shadows
knocks upon the door—
demanding entry,
demanding exit—
reflection of a darkness before.

(chorus)
That was me, this is me, this will be
until I'm gone.
The verses change, words rearrange,
but the chorus is sung on.

A voice from the echoes
shouts across the space—
demanding hearing,

demanding witness—
sound within the noise of a distant
place.

(chorus)
That was me, this is me, this will be
until I'm gone.
The verses change, words rearrange,
but the chorus is sung on.

A line from the chorus
rings within the mind—
demanding harmony,
demanding counterpoint—
a melody beneath a dissonant
rhyme.

(chorus)
That was me, this is me, this will be
until I'm gone.
The verses change, words rearrange,

but the chorus is sung on.

An image out of yesteryear
hangs within the vault—
demanding viewing,
demanding insight—
portrait of the self includes the
fault.

(chorus)
That was me, this is me, this will be
until I'm gone.
The verses change, words rearrange,
but the chorus is sung on.

A word from other stories
speaks from off the page—
demanding reading,
demanding knowing—
truth beneath the lies from a
separate stage.

(chorus)
That was me, this is me, this will be
until I'm gone.
The verses change, words rearrange,
but the chorus is sung on.

An act of ancient drama
plays out within the now—
demanding seeing,
demanding healing—
reasons for the questions why and
how.

(chorus)
That was me, this is me, this will be
until I'm gone.
The verses change, words rearrange,
but the chorus is sung on.

## About the Songwriter

**Denton Reynolds** was a New England folk-rock artist with a love of allegory and elusive lyrics. His break-out song, "Teachable Moments," about love and learning and the intricacies of teacher-student interdependence, was the title cut of his only album, a cassette release. It was a favorite of young math genius Regina Josephson. "Always Me," another cut from that album, became an anthem of historian Shanna Newsom. It opened one of the singer's last appearances, the Berkshire Buskers Music Fest in 1996.

From *The Four-Color Puzzle* (Gesher Press, 2013) and *Always Me* (Gesher Press, 2020), reprinted with permission.

## *Infinite Black*

Jolene Maples

The dead feel no pain,
Neither know they any joy.
The unborn without aim,
adrift through nameless void,
speak nothing in their silent cries.
Nothing is not,
and nothing's but a name
that darkness sighs within the night.
The nighttime leaves with a soaring
  shout,
splitting the dream with a glancing
  beam
of rising light,
only to return once again in doubt

to whisper still of unspoken fright.
The night, and night again—
endless, invincible, indifferent to
  the brief lived day between;
The night, and night again—
endless, invincible, indifferent to
  the brief lived day between.

## About the Songwriter

**Jolene Maples**, lead singer for the goth-rock band Graphene Promises, wrote "Infinite Black" after the death of her boyfriend, the group's drummer, Manny Black. After losing his adoptive mother, young genius Paolo Franzetti sang to himself the song, a favorite of one of his best friends.

From *The Intaglio Imprint* (Gesher Press, 2017), reprinted with permission.

## *Second Chance*

Astrid Gundlach

Another round, a different sound,
one more time to dance—

All I ever asked
is another at bat,
a second final act,
a second second chance.

Another walk, one more talk,
a needed bonus tranche—

All I ever asked
is another at bat,
a second final act,

a second second chance.

An extra slide, still by your side,
caught within your trance—

All I ever asked
is another at bat,
a second final act,
a second second chance.

## About the Songwriter

**Astrid Gundlach**, of Silicon Salvation, was an unclassifiable singer who hopped from metal-pop to scream-o to dub-step with hardly a pause between. Her signature across all genres was harmonic monotony, heavy on fuzz and bass beat, with limited lyrics repeated incessantly around subtle rhythmic variations thrown in at unexpected moments. "Second Chance" became a favorite of Coleman Drucker and his teenage daughter, Becca, after she played the track on her iPhone upon admitting to once again having "borrowed" from his personal marijuana stash.

From *The Drucker Proxy* (Gesher Press, 2019), reprinted with permission.

## *My Heated Heart*

Jake Norwell

Hell ain't got no heat to match the
heat that's in my heart,
And I'd gladly crawl right back to
you, if I just knew where to start.

You kicked me from the kitchen
first,
then booted me from your bed.
I could not slake my thirst for you
or push you from my head.
I flirted with the ladies when I was
a-feeling blue,
then you told me I should burn in
hell for what I done to you.

[chorus]
Hell ain't got no heat to match the
heat that's in my heart,
And I'd gladly crawl right back to
you, if I just knew where to start.

## About the Songwriter

**Jake Norwell**, a Cal-Tech dropout and front man for the country-rock trio Rodeo Rogues, spent fourteen years playing bars and road houses throughout the American Southwest before inventing a sonic cellphone hacking device that he sold to an Israeli cybersecurity company for enough to buy a ranch in Utah and retire. Few of the group's songs were memorable, but a single line from "My Heated Heart" became an internet meme when a TikTok video from a jilted bisuteki chef in Tokyo went viral. It is misquoted by internet journalist Dana Carmody on seeing her estranged father.

From *The Drucker Proxy* (Gesher Press, 2019), reprinted with permission.

## *Parallel Lines*

Chaim Hassan, Samih Sayed,
and Abdullah Sirhan

Parallel lines. Parallel lines.
Parallel lines of opposing signs,
a shouting match of repeated
attacks.
And in the middle, between,
Too subdued to be heard above the
slogans and screams,
The voices of the many all murmur
a dream.

A fanatical few invoking The Name:
faithful fundamentalists and true
reactionaries,

orthodox extremists and
revolutionaries,
True believers all distinctive
but all sounding the same.
Controlling conversation,
Reciting revelation,
Shouting new invective,
Without nuance or perspective:
Resolute truth and absolute right;
black is still black and white is
always white.
But the voices of the many all
murmur a dream.
Too subdued to be heard above the
slogans and screams,
The words and the whimpers of
those in midstream
Are lost in the chaos of the
stubborn extremes.

[voice under instrumental]
Left-center, right-center, never
centered, out.
Always stay on message so you
build your online clout.
Bark your false distinctions,
and mark your preconditions.
Measure truth in decibels, reality in
real estate;
integrity is just a pose, another
form of click-bait.

Far-left, far-right, the meanings
still stay out of sight.
Each dystopic paradise sounds alike
in sound bites,
from irate Islamophobes and angry
anti-Semites,

marketing their racism,
raising new antagonism,
to the last evangelizing, selling
   scathing schism.
From the social democrats to
   democratic socialists,
communists and capitalists,
   updating all their secret lists:
the enemies are everywhere,
everywhere, everywhere,
enemies are everywhere,
enemies are!

Parallel lines,
parallel lines of opposing signs,
a shouting match of repeated
   attacks.
And in the middle, between,

Too subdued to be heard above the
  slogans and screams,
The voices of the many all murmur
  a dream.
The voices of the many still
  murmur a dream.
The voices of the many . . .

## *Don't Look Down*

Chaim Hassan and Abdullah Sirhan

Like a river through the desert,
mountains rising from the sea,
Do you remember what you
promised then, when you
promised me?
Like the snow on sunbaked sands
or flowers flying up the sky,
Do you remember what you asked
of me when you asked me why?
Like the earth above the treetops
and the air beneath the plow,
Do you remember how we
wondered then, when we
wondered how?

DON'T LOOK DOWN!

A dark ravine, a screen unseen,
lying in between us.
—DON'T LOOK DOWN!—
But we don't know how to bridge it,
standing far apart so rigid,
angry echo from the frigid, hidden
waters below.
And we neither of us know it,
how and why we would still fear it,
but the spirit arching bright across,
a line of life too quickly lost
in deepened gloom, without the
room
for passing or returning
in a stomach-churning yearning
on a span that seems too narrow to
be crossed.

—DON'T LOOK DOWN!—
Will we drown?
*Take a step!*
No running and no crawling, and
now no further stalling,
Or pretending to the ending,
and with neither of us bending and
forever unprepared,
trying hard not to be scared to go
far beyond the hurtin'
and of everything we dared to know
always being certain.
Not by words but by our actions,
our committed retractions
of our still dividing factions.
*Take a step!*
Your side, my side,
places where we hide
from behind our wary faces,

the sole remaining traces
of our ancient shared beginnings.
We all started somewhere,
that where, over there.
—DON'T LOOK DOWN!—
A first step, another,
—DON'T LOOK DOWN!—
walking slowly like my brother or
  my father or my sister.
—DON'T LOOK DOWN!—
Stopping.
  *Take a step!*
Dropping.
  *Take a step!*
Falling, falling faster than a feather
  or a thistle,
an abyssal epistle.
—DON'T LOOK DOWN!—
  *Take a step!*

—DON'T LOOK DOWN!—

*Take a step!*

*Take a step!*

AND DON'T LOOK DOWN!

## About the Songwriters

**Chaim Hassan**, **Samih Sayed**, and **Abdullah Sirhan** were original members, along with Nadal Gershon, of the Israeli-Palestinian rap-metal fusion band Blue-Green Algae Invasion. After the group's breakup, Hassan and Sirhan went on to form touring band Innervasion. "Parallel Lines", one of the few of the original group's songs entirely in English, was later covered by Innervasion with additional lyrics by Sirhan interpolated. Although often referred to as rap, their rapid-punch lyrics—typically on overtly political themes about peace and conflict, distance and connection—intercross conventions of rap with spoken-word poetry. "Parallel Lines" played a role in the early relationship between Arab-Israeli Marwa Khaledi and Jewish Israeli-American Bini Markham. A riff on Rabbi Nachman's call to be unafraid as we cross the narrow bridge that is the world, "Don't Look Down" was Innervasion's most successful track on both SoundCloud and YouTube.

From *Flight Track* (Gesher Press, 2015) and *Exit Plans* (Gesher Press, 2020), reprinted with permission.

# About the Editor

The editor is, of course, also the author, having compiled all the material here from diverse contributors, all of whom are the same.

Lior Samson is the pen name of a former university professor who has won awards for both fiction and non-fiction writing as well as for his innovative work in industrial design. He has more than two dozen published books, including thirteen novels and two collections of short fiction. As a consultant and teacher, he has traveled the world, lived in Australia and Portugal, and served on the faculties of two international universities.

He resides in Massachusetts with his family, where he cooks creative fusion cuisine and composes serious choral music. He is a freelance journalist and photographer and one-man technical support team for the three students in his life.

The readers who write with questions, kudos, and criticism are vital parts of the dialogue he seeks to spark through his writing. He enjoys hearing from readers and appreciates those who take the time to post reviews on Amazon and elsewhere. He can be reached by email at: lior@liorsamson.com

www.ingramcontent.com/pod-product-compliance
Lightning Source LLC
LaVergne TN
LVHW051008080826
845145LV00009B/2513

* 9 7 8 1 7 3 2 6 0 9 1 5 0 *